# You and Your Rabbit

## Jean Coppendale

700028620260

QED Publishing

First published in the UK in 2004 by
QED Publishing
A Quarto Group Company
226 City Road
London, EC1V 2TT

www.qed-publishing.co.uk

A Catalogue record for this book is available from the British Library.

ISBN 1 84538 286 2

Written by Jean Coppendale
Consultant Michaela Miller
Designed by Susi Martin
Editor Gill Munton
All photographs by Jane Burton except Angora and English Lop
page 9, John Daniels/Ardea
Vegetables on page 20 by Chris Taylor
With many thanks to Jasmine Smith and Daniel Foulsham
Picture of Cuddles on page 29 by Adelle Tracy
Creative Director Louise Morley
Editorial Manager Jean Coppendale

Printed and bound in China

Words in **bold** are
explained on page 32.

# Contents

# Your first rabbit

▲ Rabbits are very cute, but they can scratch and bite.

Rabbits make lovely pets, but they do not like to be picked up or cuddled too much.

Rabbits also need a lot of looking after, because they must be kept clean and well fed.

▲ Rabbits live for six to eight years and need to be looked after every day.

▲ **Rabbits are not toys. They are small and fragile, and easily hurt.**

▶ **Rabbits enjoy having friends to live with.**

# Which rabbit?

In the wild, rabbits live in large groups. Your pet will be happier if it has a friend to live with. Two brothers or sisters from the same litter would be ideal.

## Rabbits are lovely to stroke

◀ **Long-haired rabbits, like this blue Angora, will need to be brushed every day.**

▶ **A big rabbit, like this silver and white lop-eared rabbit, may be too heavy to carry and difficult to look after.**

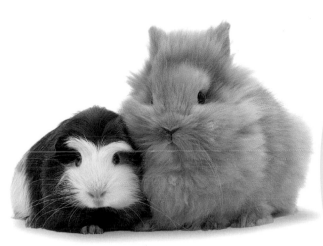

If rabbits and Guinea pigs are brought up together from when they are very young, they will get on well.

**Parent Points**

Pure-bred rabbits do not usually make good pets. It is best to get your rabbit from a rescue home, where the staff will be able to recommend a rabbit that is suitable for your circumstances.

If you buy two rabbits, make sure that both are neutered, otherwise they will fight, and keep an eye on them at first to make sure that one doesn't bully the other. Do not mix male and female rabbits as they will have babies. Rabbits do get on with cats and dogs if they are brought up together. Otherwise, keep dogs and cats well away from your rabbits!

▼ **A dwarf rabbit like this is the easiest to look after.**

# Lots of rabbits

There are lots of different **breeds** of rabbits which have different markings and colourings.

▶ Black and tan Netherland dwarf

▲ Blue Dutch rabbit

▼ Butterfly English lop-eared rabbit

◀ **Giant Angora rabbit**

▶ **Fawn English spotted rabbit**

◀ **English Lop**

9

# Rabbit shopping list

## Your rabbit will need

▶ A wooden hutch with legs so that it is off the ground

▲ A toilet tray

Your rabbit will need a bed of hay

▲ Wood shavings

▼ Hay

▲ A carrot-shaped gnawing block for the rabbit's teeth

Two water bottles, one for the hutch and one for the run, and a bottle brush

A run for the garden

Two heavy food bowls, one for the hutch and one for the run

A scoop for cleaning the hutch

A baby's hairbrush

# Getting ready

Place the hutch in a warm, quiet spot. The hutch should have a closed-off area so that the rabbit has a private place to sleep. The main part of the hutch should have an open, wire mesh front so that the rabbit can see out.

Put a layer of old newspaper on the floor of the hutch. Then put a 5-centimetre layer of wood shavings (or cat litter) on top. Make a bed of hay in the sleeping area.

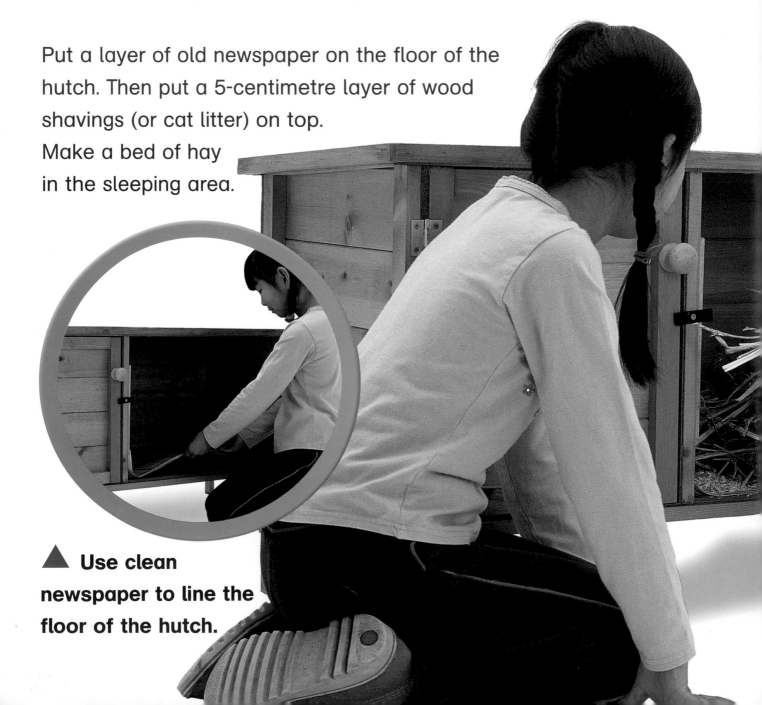

▲ **Use clean newspaper to line the floor of the hutch.**

Your rabbit should have a run in the garden. Make sure that it is big enough for the rabbit to run around in, and that it cannot be easily knocked over. Always bring the rabbit indoors at night.

◀ **Use wood shavings bought from a pet shop.**

**Parent Points**

A hutch for two small rabbits should measure at least 150cm x 60cm x 60cm. The rabbits must be able to stand up on their hind legs when they are in the hutch. Make sure the door catches are not spring-loaded, as this may injure your child or the rabbits.

Do not use clay-based cat litter in the hutch – straw-based varieties are more suitable.

An outdoor hutch must be sheltered from wind, rain and sun, and it should be raised on legs to avoid damp and to prevent insects and other animals crawling in.

# Saying hello

When your rabbit arrives, it may be feeling very scared. Place it gently in its hutch, and leave it alone for a little while so that it can get used to its new home. Rabbits like to be able to hop about. They do not like to be picked up and cuddled too much.

▶ **Talk quietly to your pet – loud noises and shouting will frighten it.**

**Parent Points**
Make sure your child knows how to handle the rabbit before he or she tries to pick it up (see pages 16–17).

House rabbits can be toilet trained. Begin by getting your pet used to the toilet tray in its hutch, and then place the tray in a quiet, draught-free room. You should be able to obtain advice on training from your rabbit's breeder or your local vet, who may also have some information leaflets.

# Handle with care

Do not pick up your rabbit unless you are sitting or kneeling down. To pick it up turn the rabbit to face you. Put one hand on the **scruff** of its neck and the other hand under its bottom. Lift the rabbit towards you. Do not let its back legs dangle.

▲ **When you stroke your pet start at its head and move down towards its bottom.**

To put your rabbit back in its hutch lower it down gently, back feet first. Never put your rabbit on a table or chair as it might fall off and hurt itself.

◀ **Let your rabbit sit on your lap. If it starts to wriggle put it down.**

**Parent Points**
Rabbits can scratch, bite and kick, so always supervise your child and the rabbit when they are together. Make sure that your child puts the rabbit down as soon as it starts to wriggle, and that he or she never runs around while holding the rabbit.

▼ **Rabbits can scratch, bite and kick, so always be very gentle when you pick it up.**

# Looking after your rabbit

Most rabbits keep their own fur clean, but they still enjoy being brushed. Use a soft baby's hairbrush and brush the fur from the rabbit's head towards its bottom.

If you think your rabbit has fleas or ticks, ask your vet for advice.

▶ **Always be gentle when you brush your rabbit.**

Give your rabbit a block of wood to gnaw on. This will help to keep its teeth short and sharp. If you think that your rabbit is having trouble chewing its food, take it to a vet. Its teeth may have grown too long and need to be looked at.

▲ **A special mineral block from a pet shop will help to keep your pet healthy.**

▲ **Make sure your rabbit has plenty of water to drink at all times, both indoors and outdoors.**

**Parent Points**

If the rabbit has a runny nose or runny eyes, or if its fur looks dull and dry, take it to the vet. Check your rabbit's claws and teeth regularly to make sure that they are not too long. They may need to be trimmed by the vet.

Rabbits should have regular vaccinations – check with your local vet. During warm weather check your rabbit for flystrike – fly eggs or maggots in the fur.

# Feeding your rabbit

Feed your rabbit special rabbit food from a pet shop. It will also like slices of fresh vegetables such as cabbage, watercress, carrots and plantain. Your rabbit will enjoy being fed.

◀ **Make sure your rabbit always has clean food to eat.**

**Baby corns**

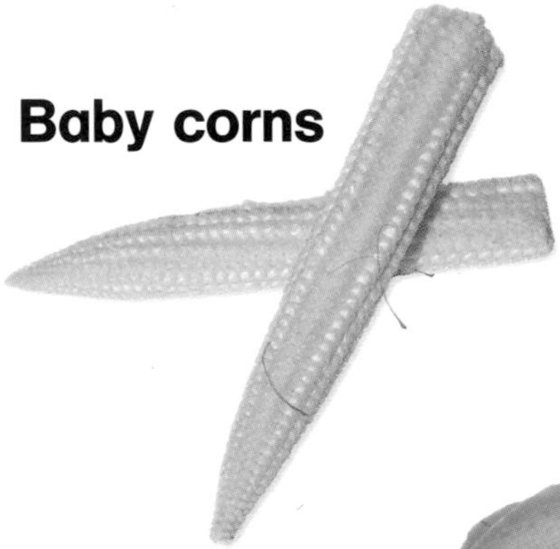

**Carrot**

**Celery**

Your rabbit will enjoy nibbling herbs such as mint and parsley, and dandelion leaves. Make sure you do not pick the dandelion leaves in a place where there is a lot of traffic or where people walk their dogs.

**Parent Points**
Fresh food should always be washed before it is given to the rabbit. Do not give rabbits lettuce or fresh fruit because they are bad for their digestion.

◀ **Feed your rabbit fresh vegetables about three times a week.**

# Keep it clean

Your rabbit's hutch needs to be kept clean.
Once a day, clear out any droppings and
dirty or wet bedding, and remove any old
bits of food. Put in some clean bedding
of fresh hay.

Wash the food bowls every day, and make sure your rabbit always has clean water to drink.

Once or twice a week, clean out the hutch thoroughly. Wipe it down with water and disinfectant. Throw away all the old newspaper, wood shavings and hay, and replace them with fresh, clean bedding.

▲ **Clean your pet's water bottles with a bottle brush once a week.**

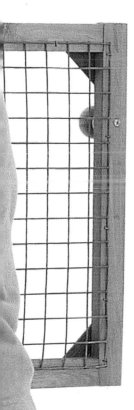

◀ **Always wash your hands after you have cleaned the hutch.**

**Parent Points**
Use animal-safe disinfectant (available from pet shops) for cleaning the hutch. If the water bottle has a ball bearing, make sure it isn't jammed.

# Your rabbit's life cycle

(4)

▲ When a female rabbit is about four months old she is old enough to have babies.

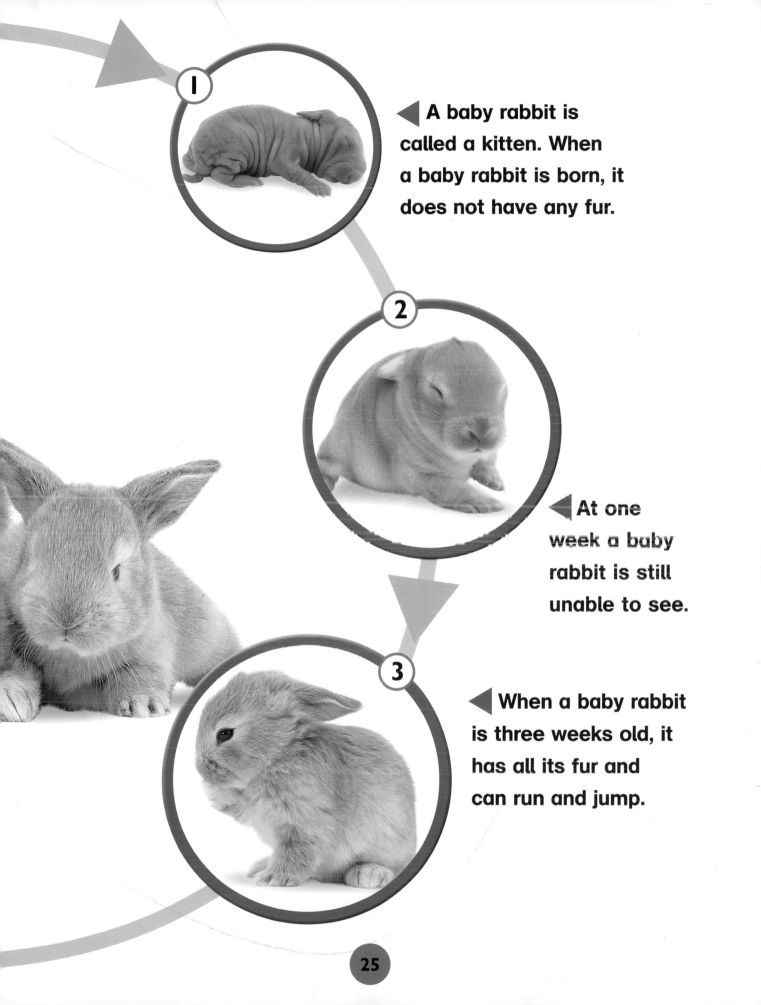

◀ **A baby rabbit is called a kitten. When a baby rabbit is born, it does not have any fur.**

◀ **At one week a baby rabbit is still unable to see.**

◀ **When a baby rabbit is three weeks old, it has all its fur and can run and jump.**

# Let's play!

You can make an exciting rabbit playground from old cardboard boxes and baskets. Put in some old toys and hay.

When your pet is in its outdoor run, hide some hay in an overturned flowerpot – or scatter bits of rabbit food on the floor of the hutch for it to find.

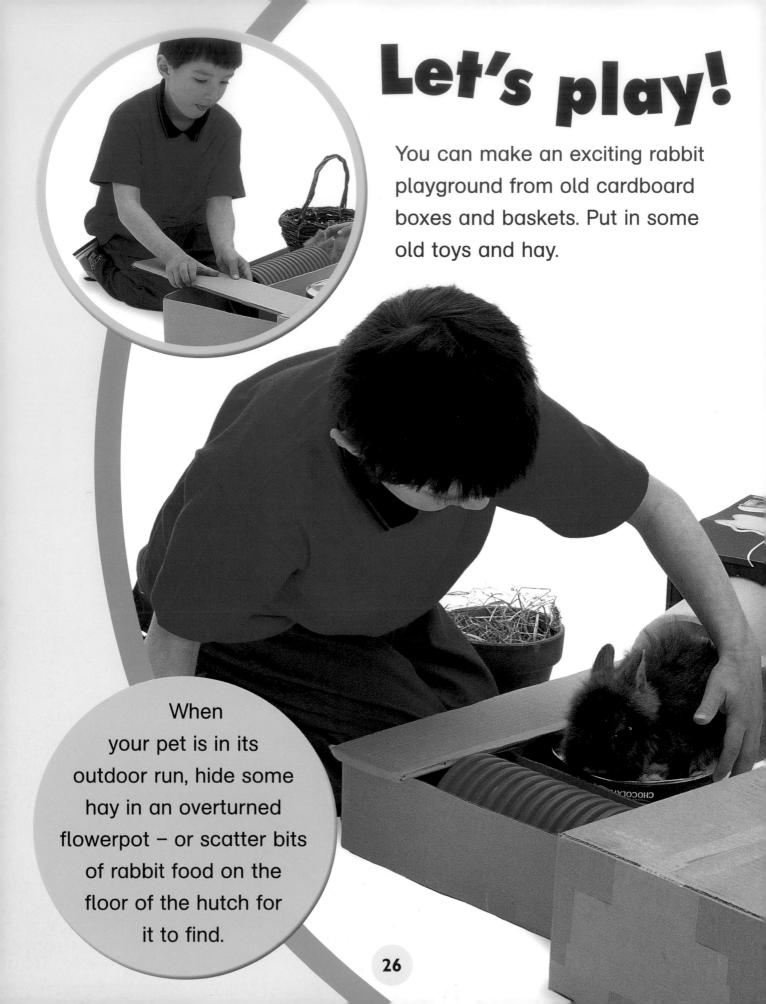

**Parent Points**

If your child is playing with the rabbit in the garden, make sure that the area is safe. The rabbit must not be able to escape. It is also important to check that no cats or dogs are nearby. Indoors, make sure that your home is 'rabbit-proof', as rabbits like to chew electrical wires and furniture.

# Saying goodbye

As your rabbit grows older, it will spend more and more time sleeping. Make sure it is warm, safe and cosy. It may need help to keep its fur clean and its nails short.

Cuddles last summer

◀ If your pet sounds as if it is not breathing properly, tell an adult immediately.

**Parent Points**

A very sick rabbit may need to be put to sleep. This will need sensitive handling.

If your child's rabbit dies, let him or her cry and express sadness. Writing a story about the pet – or putting together a scrapbook or montage of photos and drawings – can be very therapeutic.

It is not always a good idea to replace the pet immediately – let your child grieve first.

My pet Cuddles

# Remember all the fun you had together

If your pet is very old or ill, it may die. Try not to be too sad, but remember all the fun you had together. You may want to bury your pet in the garden, but you can take it to the vet if you prefer.

# Rabbit checklist

Read this list, and think about all the points.

✔ **Rabbits are not toys.**

✔ Treat your rabbit gently – as you would like to be treated yourself.

✔ A rabbit may live for 12 years – will you get bored with your pet?

✔ **How will you treat your rabbit if it makes you angry?**

✔ **Never hit your pet, shout at it or throw things at it.**

✔ **Animals feel pain, just as you do.**

✔ Will you be happy to clean out your pet's hutch every day?

# Parents' checklist

- You, not your child, are responsible for the care of the rabbits.

- If you go on holiday, you will need a responsible person to come and feed, clean and exercise the rabbit, or take them to a holiday home.

- It's best to keep two rabbits, as they like to live in groups.

- Rabbits need plenty of exercise. Ideally, a rabbit owner should have a garden.

- Rabbits should not be left alone all day.

- Can you afford a good-sized hutch for the house and a run for the garden, food, bedding and vet's bills?

- The hutch will need to be kept in a quiet place, away from draughts and direct sunshine.

- Rabbits can kick, bite and scratch, and are not suitable pets for very young children.

- Rabbits do not like to be held or cuddled for a long time.

- If your child gets bored with cleaning out the hutch every day, it will become your job. Are you prepared for this?

- Always supervise pets and children.

# Rabbit words

A rabbit can twitch its **nose**.

A rabbit has long **ears**.

A rabbit's fur is called its **coat**.

Rabbits have a small tail, called a **bob tail**.

The long hairs on a rabbit's face are called **whiskers**.

A rabbit has **claws** on its toes.

A **breed** is a special type of rabbit, such as a Blue Dutch or Fawn English Spotted.

The rabbit's **scruff** is the area at the back of its neck.

# Index